A Little Thing Called

"ATTITUDE"

10 Dynamic Lessons to Supercharge Your Life

Sam Glenn

"The Attitude Guy"

Copyright © 2023

Need some real inspiration, go check out my videos at: www.SamGlenn.com.

(It's worth two minutes of your time - I promise.)

Attitude Changes Everything Book Series ©

eBook ISBN: 978-969-3792-20-1

Paperback ISBN: 978-969-3792-21-8

Hardback ISBN: 978-969-3792-22-5

Your ATTITUDE is that little thing that makes a big difference in every way, in everything, every day!"

- Sam Glenn

Table of Contents

Introduction

(Would you rather watch a *video introduction*?

Go to: SamGlennBOOKS.com and click on books.

I will be there waiting for you!

****

If you are reading this book, I truly believe you are an attitude warrior. Meaning, YOU GET IT! You celebrate the impact and gift of your attitude. So, why read a book about attitude? I think you will agree that even the best of us sometimes our attitude gets off track, and we need something to nudge us. Sometimes, it's a refreshing reminder of something we already know. Sometimes we just need a little encouragement to not give up, to try again, and to keep going. The words on the following pages are designed to bring you strength, empowerment, and feed your attitude. This is a classroom of lessons that have helped me improve and shift my attitude from the liability column to the asset column. If you are reading this book, I truly believe you care about bettering your life and value the incredible role your attitude plays in your life every day.

Let's be real about this attitude stuff. In the course of a day, we don't really sit around and think about our attitude in great depth. However, your attitude is present all day, every day. It never takes a break and is either working for you or against you, and only you can determine which.

Throughout this book, I will share some valuable "attitude lessons" from real life experiences. Some of those experiences are humbly less than ideal moments, but we all have them and the value to you and I is they offer us an incredible platform to learn and grow. I will also highlight how our attitude can reward us through awareness, practice, and being intentional.

Being positive doesn't mean you don't ever have negative thoughts. It just means you don't allow those thoughts to control your life.

Cultivating an attitude that effectively works for you in positive ways is more than saying or thinking, "Think positive. Be positive. Live positive." There are some super simple steps you can take that will build up the right kind of momentum and direct your attitude into more rewarding outcomes.

If you want your life to get better, it truly starts when you get better, and that starts with one single choice–choosing a better attitude.

If there is one little life lesson that sticks with me every day, it is that our attitude plays a giant role in every aspect of our life. Your attitude impacts your health, finances, relationships, and work.

- A better attitude makes your skills work better.

- A better attitude makes you better.

- It makes your life better.

And if you are reading this book, I am pretty sure you don't have to be sold on that simple truth. However, the goal is to keep fueling the right attitude in the right direction to achieve the right outcomes. That is what our time will reflect in the following pages. I promise, it will be worth it.

While this book is a very quick read, I happen to believe it is mighty. When you put this information into action, it will create a consistent and mighty impact in your life and those you care about. Think of this book like ordering an espresso instead of a big cup of coffee. The espresso may be small, but it sure packs a mighty kick.

And lastly, if you ever need a little encouragement or what I like to call a positive kick in the attitude, be sure to watch some of my videos at: SamGlenn.com.

"They're so good!"

– Sam's Daughter

Also, if you enjoy this book, check out my other books on Amazon or SamGlennBOOKS.com.

"My dad's books are like really amazingly good! I read them to fall asleep faster at bedtime."

– Sam's other Daughter

Remember, your attitude is your choice, and it is and will always be that little thing that makes a big difference!

FREE STUFF TIME!!!

(As Iron Sharpens Iron…This is Going to Be

EPIC!)

#ACE

How would you like to get some really cool "free stuff" and make an unforgettable difference for thousands of your fellow humans?

I am looking for a few inspiring "attitude warriors" who can help me with a special "**Attitude Changes Everything**" Project (#ACE) because it will impact thousands of lives for the better…including yours.

"This project isn't a Sam Glenn thing, but rather a YOU and I thing. As iron sharpens iron, let's do something remarkable together!"

Okay, here are a few very simple actions to get some really cool stuff and make a life changing difference.

Step 1:

(5 Minutes or less) Leave a five star "inspiring" review for this book on Amazon.

HOWEVER...

DO NOT leave a normal or typical review as you would for a book, but one that communicates "YOUR" personal inspiration as to why having a better attitude makes life, family, relationships, health, and work better. This is your time to inspire and allow your testimonial to encourage others in the direction of a better and happier life.

Fill it in, *"A better attitude makes life better because...."*

                www.SamGlenn.com

Everyone has a story. I have a story; you have a story, and we are contributors to these stories every day. This is your chance to help co-author a story that makes a difference for someone who really needs it. Maybe someone is lost like I once was and just needs some healthy encouragement. Maybe it's someone who has an A+ optimistic attitude and they just need something healthy to feed their mind. So, your review should be one that inspires. The goal is to turn the review section into a feed of strength, encouragement, and inspiration.

NO OTHER BOOK HAS EVER DONE THIS.

This will be a first.

If it works, it will be EPIC.

All you have to do is take a few minutes and write a few sentences as to why having a better attitude makes a difference to you. (It should take you less than five minutes to achieve this task, but if you want, take your time, and share your testimonial, because it will live on forever. How cool is that?"

Step 2:

Once your review posts, which sometimes can take a day or two, take a screenshot and email it to Amanda@SamGlenn.com. She is my super incredible assistant who loves giving away free stuff. In exchange for sharing your inspiration, she will send you a digital eBook of one of my favorite books, Not All Superheroes Wear Capes. I absolutely love this book! In addition, she will send you a super awesome digital print of my artwork that you can print and frame. These are some of my favorite things that bring joy, encouragement, and inspiration to others.

My artwork will brighten any room or workplace and this book will make you want to binge watch superhero movies - it's really good!! (If you are leader in your organization, share the files with your team at a team meeting. Pop some popcorn, put on one of my videos and then let everyone know you are giving them a digital copy of my book. How fun would that be at your next staff meeting? Heck, if you are making popcorn, I may show up.)

To anyone doubting my intentions, this part is for you...

$$$

So, this may seem like I am asking for reviews to make more books sales and guess what, I am! And here is why-because I donate book sales to an organization called Make a Wish Foundation (Wish.org). They help grant incredible dreams for boys and girls who are experiencing cancer or life threating illnesses. So, for a few of your inspirational words, you get something cool in return, but as iron sharpens iron, we come together in an effort to make a difference for others. How amazing is that?

Imagine going to your favorite sporting event or even a Taylor Swift concert and being in a giant stadium with fans just like you who are celebrating something special. It reminds me of one of my favorite quotes, "The strength of the wolf is in the pack and the strength of the pack is in the wolf."

I love that quote because we truly are stronger when we come together for a common and lifechanging purpose.

Let's support each other even more – beyond a review. While social media says hashtags are a thing of the past, let's communicate and support each other through this hashtag *#ACE* which stands for *Attitude Changes Everything.* When you post something inspiring, uplifting, pure, positive, supportive and encouraging, add that hashtag so other attitude warriors can find you, support you and join in.

!!!WARNING!!!

Please note, if all this does catch on and goes viral, remember there are those who make it their mission to turn good things bad. They use their words in negative ways and go out of their way to minimize the efforts of a good mission. These are people who choose to plant misery and want others to be sad, down, toxic and miserable. I believe life already has enough of that stuff, so we as attitude warriors are not contributors to this platform. We don't share hate or go out of way to make others feel bad. We are too busy make the most of our most precious gift – time. We don't waste it making life miserable for others. We lift others up!

So, what is the solution when others aren't kind, supportive and communicate in ways that knock others down? We forge on – together! We demonstrate love, kindness, respect and set an example that perhaps may influence someone to rethink their attitude and actions. You just never know. There was a time when I used to be very toxic and negative. I changed. I discovered thinking and living in a toxic way doesn't make life better, so I started a new path for my life and here I am.

Finally, thank you to all the attitude warriors out there who share in this mission to make life a little better for others. I appreciate you and am rooting for you!

We are stronger together!

Sam Glenn

#ACE - Attitude Changes Everything

www.SamGlenn.com

Attitude Lesson #1
Your Attitude Becomes What You Feed It

(Quotes from The Whiteboard)

I remember in a conversation with my late mentor, Zig Ziglar, he asked me, and I am paraphrasing here, "Sam, if you had a million-dollar racehorse, would you feed it junk food, let it drink booze, and stay up all night?"

Of course, I wouldn't treat a million-dollar racehorse that way, but his point was very clear that what we feed our mind is what our mind grows or develops into. Zig said, "You have a billion-dollar brain, so why would you feed your mind something that isn't good for you?"

I have always enjoyed and found value from Mr. Ziglar's insights. So, I ask you, what are you feeding your billion-dollar brain?

Our thoughts show up in our attitude, actions, and choices. One thing Mr. Ziglar shared that inspired me to feed my mind better was, "Sam, if you don't like the output in your life, you need to change the input. Input creates output. Feed your mind good stuff. Read good books. Listen to good audios. Surround yourself with good people who bring out your best."

He is right. I acted on his wisdom, and it changed my life for the better. Since, I wasn't a big reader during my initial interactions with Mr. Ziglar, he encouraged me to start small by reading good quotes daily. Guess what I love doing every day now? Reading good quotes! They are seriously like vitamins for your attitude. It requires less than 30 seconds to read a good quote, but it can fuel a better mindset for a day or help you stay optimistic and resilient through a challenging situation. Some quotes stay with you for a lifetime. Do you have an all-time favorite good quote? If you share your favorite quote on your social media, tag me @samglenn or @samglennspeaker so I can like, comment, and share.

Honestly, I think sometimes we just get so busy with life and work and forget to feed our attitude. Instead of thinking of feeding your attitude like work, make it a routine that you enjoy and look forward to daily. For example, when I wake up, I make a cup of coffee and take a few minutes to read a couple of quotes to feed my mind. If I read one that I absolutely love, I share it on social media. But, as you can see, this isn't something I have to do, it is rather something I look forward to doing. There is a big difference.

I think when you change the experience of betterment, it makes all the difference in the world. When it becomes something you look forward to, you get excited and make it a priority. It gets bumped up instead of bumped out. The key is you have to make your betterment process unique to you but also make it something you authentically get excited about. What a difference that will make in your life.

Quotes from The Whiteboard

The year was 1994, and I was nearing graduation from college. The university hosted a large job fair and after two hours of what I would call really bad interviews, I ended up landing a three-month internship with the largest, most prestigious company in their industry. The interview line seemed like a mile long because everyone from my university wanted to work for this organization and get the bragging and branding rights of the company's name on their resume. Typically, they hired at most, two students a year to work at their company. It was no easy task to get hired by them, but everyone was up for the challenge.

I will admit I wasn't overly enthusiastic about getting a job and participating in the real world. That is how everyone put it, "Are you ready for the real world?"

I wasn't. I was content with taking my time. So, when I landed this internship, I was really surprised. In fact, when fellow classmates discovered this very prestigious company hired me, it literally catapulted me into a minor celebrity status on our college campus.

Everyone looked at me differently and wanted to know exactly what I said and did during my interview. Some of my closer classmates inspected my resume, my clothes, and what kind of toothpaste I used. Everyone was looking for a key in the door. I guess they thought I had it.

(Honestly, I really believe what got me in the door to work for this company was my attitude. But not just an up-beat proactive type of attitude. It was something special. In the next chapter, I will share one of my favorite attitudes–lightheartedness. In fact, it's a signature part of the speeches I give today.

What happened was the person who was doing the interviewing seemed exhausted. I really didn't think they would hire me, but I stood in line with my classmates like waiting to ride a rollercoaster at the theme park. When it was my turn, I said, "I think I got in the wrong line."

The interviewer was like, "Well, since you are here, let's see what you got."

I don't remember exactly what I said in the interview, but I remember making her laugh, a lot.

Everyone standing in line waiting to be interviewed looked confused because the interaction didn't come across like a standard job interview. I remember one guy looked so annoyed like he thought I was wasting everyone's time.

I didn't feel any pressure because I had no expectation of landing a job with this company, so I was my natural self. When the interview ended, the person who interviewed me said, "Sam, thank you. I needed this today. You made my day. I haven't laughed like that in such a long time."

I was hired.

All this attention I was receiving made me think that perhaps this is a pretty big deal. Maybe I can learn something of value from this organization. Who would have thought I was getting excited about a real-world job.

DAY ONE

"What did I get myself into?!!"

On my first day of "real world" work, I was nervous and excited. I thought, "If this is the best company in the world, then they must have the best people in the world."

That was only an assumption and not a good one. Before I continue the tale of this adventure, I want to point out a very crucial lesson – especially to leaders reading this book. When you stop doing what contributes to success, success is no longer possible. *(Underline that last sentence and reread it often).* That insight is true for anything in life. I heard a quote the other day, which I absolutely love, "Don't complain about the results you didn't get from the work you didn't do."

Isn't that so good?

My point in sharing this part of the story is to highlight that this once prestigious company that dominated their industry no longer exists. The leadership stopped cultivating a caring culture and eventually when enough people stop caring, everything collapses. Eventually, this Goliath company crumbled to the ground (metaphorically) and turned back into dust. Remember, the absence of care is collapse.

My first day was a shocker. It was filled with unpleasant and disappointing surprises. First, the attitude of everyone I encountered or observed was less than inspiring. The vibe was toxic. It made you want to ask, "Did something bad happen?"

You got the impression that nobody really cared. It felt like a group of people working for a paycheck rather than a purpose. My boss was always yelling at people and belittling them. I remember thinking, "What did I get myself into?"

Here is another saying, "It is not the water around the boat that sinks the boat, but the water we let in it."

This internship sank my attitude fast. I became my work environment. I modeled the "I don't care" attitude from my fell co-workers. I cut corners, showed up late, left early, let the phone go to voicemail, and became an example of disengagement. I felt sick going to work. I became moody and short tempered with others. I would make excuses to call in sick. The bottom line, it wasn't what I thought, and it wasn't good.

Here is where the story changes. And that is the beauty of any circumstance, we can change the story when we change the attitude we bring to the story.

One day, I answered the phone with about as much enthusiasm as paint drying. I may have also been in the middle of a 30-minute daydream. However, it was a familiar voice. It was my mom, who wasn't initially sure it was me. She wasn't used to hearing her boy sound like a zombie. She asked if I was okay or if I needed help. I laughed and thought, "Yes! Save me! S.O.S. I am sick of this job, I am sick from this job and I have only been here 27 days."

When I informed my mom that I wasn't sick or needed immediate help, she began to educate me or lecture me on how she brought me up to answer a phone the right way. She was right. I actually had the best training in the world when it came to answering phones. My grandma owned and operated a successful answering service out of her home for 30 years. I loved hanging out in the room with all the phones. I learned firsthand at an early age how to answer the phone with a smile, have a conversation, and communicate well. People can feel your attitude over the phone. That was my early real life work training. And it was good.

However, in this situation, I simply abandoned my training. My negative attitude had more influence over me than my optimistic attitude. My environment was so toxic that I was physically and mentally exhausted at the end of the day. And I really didn't even do much if that gives you any indication why cultivating a healthy workplace environment is so vital. Yes, VITAL.

SUNDAY DINNER AT MOM'S HOUSE

"You got me a gift from a garage sale?"

It was over Sunday dinner at my mom's house, she gifted me with a desktop calendar. I remember thinking, "Oh joy, workplace stuff."

She had purchased this desktop calendar from a garage sale. It wasn't even the right year. So, I inquired, "Mom, why did you purchase a calendar from years ago?"

She said, "Samuel, forget the dates. I didn't get it for that reason. Read the quotes under the date. Under every date is an uplifting quote. I thought of you when I saw this. I want you to put this on your desk and read these little quotes daily to see if they help you feel better and happier."

My mom has always been a joyful encourager.

"Samuel, you may not have the best job in the world, but you can make the best of your job and make it better. It starts with a little thing called your attitude. Now, go wash your hands for dinner."

I was reluctant to bring this outdated calendar to work, but I followed through. I was in the middle of sorting papers and quicky glanced over at the calendar. I leaned forward to read the quote, "If you can look up, you can get up!" by Les Brown.

I started to repeat the quote out loud because I wasn't sure exactly what it meant. But, I am not joking when I say this, after repeating it over 30 times, I got it! I felt a shift in my thoughts and attitude. I was like, "What just happened?!!"

I felt energy. I felt like my attitude got a B12 shot! So, I started flipping through the calendar and reading more quotes. The more quotes I read, the more my mind changed for the better. I felt less sick and more motivated to do my work in a way that would make my mom proud. Heck, I was proud. That is a good feeling, when you can work hard and be proud of the work you do.

The quotes didn't change the fact that I was working in a toxic environment, but the quotes changed me and how I worked in a less than ideal environment. Do you see the difference a little thing called attitude can make?

ENTER THE WHITEBOARD

"Time to take this thing to a new level."

I noticed there was a huge whiteboard by my desk that was never used. So, I got some markers and started writing the quotes from the calendar onto the whiteboard. I didn't think anyone would mind, and they didn't. But, then something incredible happened. Everyone started stopping by my desk just to read the quotes I was putting up. After they read the quote, they would smile, shake their head in agreement, and actually be pleasant.

I noticed that it was changing the temperature of the attitude where I worked. Here is a good insight, we may not be able to control certain things in life, but we are always in charge of our attitude. Change your attitude, and you discover that you can change stories, experiences, feelings, choices, behaviors, and outcomes. I don't know about you, but that's a dynamic thought if you think about it.

The environment in our department changed. I noticed my co-workers were nicer, calmer, and willing to be helpful. I think being shocked by this outcome and new direction of our workplace environment is an understatement.

One day, when I was returning from lunch, there were a few gentlemen in really nice suits standing by my desk reading the quotes. I got the impression they played important roles in the company.

When I walked up to my desk, they turned and introduced themselves. I don't remember their names, but I remember words like vice president, executive and from the top floor. My eyes bugged out. At first, I thought I was in trouble, but they shared how they heard about my quotes on the whiteboard and how it has impacted the department. I felt important and valuable in that moment. It was a big difference from the day when my mom called me asking me if I needed help.

They complimented me on my quotes and helping improve the workplace. It was a moment I am still proud of to this day. However, the time had come, and my internship was complete. The turnaround in my attitude was like night and day. The impact on my department was like night and day. In fact, I was offered a full-time job, which I declined. I just felt like

I wanted to experience new adventures. The experience changed me, and I was ready to move on.

On my final internship day, they threw a huge party for me in the conference room. It was packed and decorated so nicely. I mean it was impressive. They never threw parties for anyone like this, so it was special and as luck would have it – I LOVE CAKE!

A few people got up to give a toast, and everyone commented on my attitude and the quotes from the whiteboard. They remarked how the quotes would help them get through a tough day or how it inspired them to do better at work.

In fact, the department supervisor who always seemed like she was in a bad mood, got up to give the final toast. She announced that she was pregnant and said, "Sam, I am so sad to see you go. Working with you gave us all something and someone to look forward to each day. I don't know if I will be having a girl or a boy, but I know I can raise this child to be as kind and thoughtful as you."

A little thing called attitude can really make a big difference.

Feeding your attitude can be life changing. Make the time so you look forward to each day and feed your attitude something that makes you better every day. That is the gift you give yourself. And a better attitude is a gift to others–those you work with, those you serve through your work, and your family. I recommend reading good quotes, keep it simple and just allow the words and the meaning to sink in. Input creates output. When you feed your attitude good things, you think better, do better, and feel better. Now, you know why I love quotes. They are attitude changers!

Attitude Lesson #2
Use Your Attitude for Good

Have you ever heard that saying that some people are a blessing and some are a lesson? How you use your attitude can determine blessings or lessons. All you have to do is reference your examples. Can you think of anyone that really made a difference in your life? That is a blessing. That is an example worth replicating. Now, can you think of anyone that made life more challenging for you? That is a lesson. That is an example of what not to do.

Just the other day, I listened to a podcast, and the guest shared that we all experience brokenness. In that brokenness, we can choose to become a villain or a hero. The villain wants to break others, so they do and speak hurtful things. The hero uses their brokenness to help others in their time of brokenness.

I believe there is more value in using your attitude for good than not.

I heard a humorous yet enlightening perspective about a woman's husband who passed. She went to the local newspaper office to put his obituary in the paper. The person helping her asked what she would like to say in the obituary. She said, "Herb is dead."

She was then informed that there was still available space to add more details if she wanted. So, the widow thought for a bit and said, "Herb is dead. Boat for sale."

Think about it, when you leave a room, are people grateful you visited or excited to see you go? Your attitude is that little thing that can be used to do good things. It's how you do your work. It's the words you use. It's how you listen, respond and act. Your attitude is always at work, so make it work in good ways.

Think about it this way, everyone you encounter has a story, and every day you have the opportunity to contribute to those stories with the incredible gift of who you are. You can be kind, understanding, attentive, compassionate, patient, empathetic, and thoughtful. But it all starts with your attitude. If you have ever attended one of my speeches, I love to use a lot of humor. I use my humorous attitude to make someone's story a little brighter. Here is one of my favorite stories and an example of how our attitude can truly make a big difference.

A few years ago, there was a woman by the name of Mary who had a heart attack and was in the hospital recovering. She is one of my super fans and has an amazing sense of humor. However, this was her third heart attack in 10 years. A friend of Mary's reached out to me to see if I wouldn't mind calling Mary and sharing a few uplifting words with her.

"Absolutely!" I said.

I called Mary in her hospital room, and she was so happy to hear from me. She seemed weak, and her voice was very faint. I said, "Mary, you know I collect and share funny stories, so I have one that my grandma shared with me, and I would love to share it with you."

She loved the story and laughed so much that she told me before we hung up, "Sam, this is the best heart attack I have ever had!"

I couldn't help laughing out loud!

Now, before I share this same story that I shared with Mary, I want to encourage you not to misinterpret this story or view it as a religious story or anything negative. Just don't make it an option. Give yourself permission to simply enjoy. Laugh if you feel the urge. I do every time I read it. Like I tell my audiences in my speeches, it's just a good old-fashioned dysfunctional story that just happens to be hilarious. And if you see it as anything else, you should reread this book at a minimum of one hundred times.

This is a story of an eighty-eight-year-old Grandma who still drives her own car. And the following is a letter to her granddaughter.

Dear Granddaughter,

The other day I went to our local Christian bookstore and saw a 'Honk if you Love Jesus' bumper sticker...

I was feeling particularly good that day because I had just come from a thrilling choir performance followed by a thunderous prayer meeting. So, I bought the sticker and put it on my bumper. I am so glad I did. What an uplifting experience that followed!

I stopped at a red light at a very busy intersection, just lost in thought about the Lord and how good he has been.

I didn't notice that the light had changed. It's a good thing someone else loves the Lord because if this person hadn't honked, I never would have noticed. In fact, I found that lots of people love Jesus! Everybody behind me was honking!

While I was sitting there, the guy behind me started honking like crazy, and then he leaned out of his window and screamed, "For the love of God! 'Go! Go! Go!"

What an exuberant cheerleader he was for the Lord! The honking continued. I just leaned out my window and started waving and celebrating with all those God-loving people. I even honked my horn a few times to share the fun! There must have been a man from Florida back there because I heard him yell something about a sunny beach!

I saw another guy waving with only his middle finger stuck up in the air. I asked my young teenage grandson in the back seat what it meant, he smiled and said, "Grandma, it's probably the Hawaiian good luck sign or something."

Well, I have never been to Hawaii, so I leaned out the window and gave him the Hawaiian good luck sign right back.

My grandson burst out laughing, even he was enjoying this wonderful experience!!!

A couple of the people were so caught up in the joy of the moment that they got out of their cars and started walking briskly towards me. I bet they wanted to ask what church I attended, but this was when I noticed the light had changed.

So, grinning, I waved at all my brothers and sisters and drove on through the intersection. I noticed that I was the only car that got through the intersection before the light changed again and felt kind of sad that I had to leave them after all the love we had shared.

So, I slowed the car down, leaned out the window and gave everyone the Hawaiian good luck sign one last time as I drove away. Will write again soon,

Love, Grandma

The moral of this story: We can use humor to lift others up.

Laughter truly is the best medicine in life. Let's explore humor a little more because it has so many benefits.

Attitude Lesson #3
Humor Prevents Hardening of the Attitude

Occasionally, we all need reminders about what is really important in life. While, humor and the ability to laugh is one of life's greatest gifts, it is also healthy for you. It is easy to let stress build up and turn our attitude sour. A little humor can bring a dose of balance, relaxation, energy, and positivity to your day.

Humor is Like Sunshine on a Cloudy Day

I was watching a documentary about Joan Rivers, and in one of the scenes, this guy who was in Joan Rivers' audience stood up offended about what she was saying and walked out, yelling why he was offended. His reasoning and outburst were uncalled for. However, I loved what Joan did next; she fired back at him and called him out. "Humor is the only thing that helps us deal with life's hard times."

She said, "My husband lost his leg in the war and had to live with that for years. When he finally got a sense of humor, he returned and got it!"

Everyone started laughing when she shared that. She has a point. There is a time to laugh and a time to hold off on laughing. It is about timing.

The moral of the story: Relax and lighten up. You will never look back on your life and wish you had laughed less. Am I right? You won't, so relax and enjoy a healthy laugh from time to time. The best laughter is pure and positive, and nobody ever feels bad because of it. Those are the rules to getting all the benefits from good humor.

Collect Funny Stories

One of the ways I nurture a healthy sense of humor is by collecting funny stories. I have my own personal collection from personal experiences, but every so often I stumble upon a story love sharing it with others to share in a good laugh. Here is a favorite...

Wrong Way

A senior citizen was driving down the freeway when his wife called his cell phone. "Herman, I just heard on the news that there's a car going the wrong way on Route 69. Please be careful!" "It's not just one car," said Herman, "It's hundreds of them!"

Humor Melts Away Stress, Calories, and Negativity

Too much of the wrong kind of stress makes your neck feel tight and thickens your blood. It can make you feel sick. Stress builds up in life, but sometimes the best outlet is a little laughter. Laughter oxygenates the body, refreshes the mind, fights off anxiety and depression, and even burns unwanted calories. The heaviest thing we carry in life is the stress we allow ourselves to carry. Too much stress is unhealthy and causes illness, fatigue, depression, and other ailments. We need a way to dump the stress, and a little humor, which can lead to laughter, is the best medicine.

I think we all have moments in our day that can be stressful. But, I also believe maybe the magical touch of humor can transform our tension into a mini vacation. I know it can. I am living proof of this.

Humor has the health-promoting power to create wellness in your life. When you laugh or have a lightened-up mood, the human body releases endorphins into your system. Endorphins are a group of chemicals that reduce pain, contribute to healthy sleep, improve the quality of moods, and heal the body.

The opposite happens when you let the tension build up. When your body suppresses negative emotions, you are at a higher risk for illness, anxiety, depression, mood swings, anger, and frustration. When you allow yourself to live in a state with limited "humor activity," you can age more quickly and become less attractive. We don't need validation of those claims to not want that. Envision someone who is really uptight versus someone who is laughing, enjoying good humor, and smiling. Who might you say appears to have more appeal?

Hands down, the person who is using their humor attitude wins.

Another benefit to having a good sense of humor is that it will give you the coping power to deal with whatever life throws your way. It does not mean that you will avoid all negative emotions. It means that your body and mind will help you respond more favorably to combat your thoughts and moods with emotions such as hope, joy, love, optimism, and caring.

According to Dr. Bill Fry at Stanford University, laughing 200 times burns off the same amount of calories as 10 minutes on a rowing machine. Laughter oxygenates your blood, increases energy, and relaxes your muscles. Studies show that laughter also strengthens your immune system.

Many hospitals today are incorporating what is known as "laugh therapy" or "humor programs." The purpose is to help in a speedy recovery. Do you remember the movie Patch Adams and how he used humor to lift people's spirits? Patch felt that it was a necessary part of healing. Today, hospital beds are filled with people who have stress-related illnesses. That is why I promote humor wherever I go.

Attitude Lesson #4
You Determine How Your Attitude Will Work – For You or Against You

Let me start with a compelling quote and observation by Holocaust survivor Victor E. Frankl, *"Everything can be taken from a man but one thing: The last of the human freedoms—to choose one's attitude in any given set of circumstances."*

That is such a powerful quote. Only one person can choose your attitude in any circumstance; that person is you! You are the CEO of your attitude. Your attitude works and operates the way you propose it to work. It will be your greatest superpower or weakness—it's up to you. But remember this, whatever attitude you choose... everything follows it—*your choices, thoughts, efforts, behaviors, communication, responses, and actions.* That awareness alone is a game changer. Everything follows your attitude.

Welcome to Attitude University

In 1995, I had just graduated college but surprisingly did not feel smarter. I took the scenic route to receive my diploma by cramming four years of college into five. As humorous and truthful as that is, I was more confused when I graduated than when I started school. My mind was overwhelmed with fear, doubt, and anxiety.

After our graduation ceremony, I sat on my mom's couch in a daze and blurted out, "WHAT NEXT???"

I have always had a creative and entrepreneurial spirit since I was a young boy or under six feet tall. I have been self-employed since 1998, which to me feels like a miracle despite a recession, pandemic, unethical people, and a million other little challenges. Sometimes, I wake up and think, "How in the world did I make it this far?"

I will answer that question in the following pages.

From 1995-1997 I got by doing various odd jobs, ranging from delivering newspapers, cleaning floors, and working the graveyard shift. It was work, but those jobs weren't my ultimate calling. After graduating college, I was up to my eyeballs in debt and couldn't afford a place on my own, so I slept on my mom's living room floor or sometimes in my '82 Buick Regal.

As time began to pass, my question shifted from "What next?" to "When will things get better?"

Every day it felt like I was running on a treadmill and getting nowhere fast. I honestly believe that one of the worst feelings in the world is waking up without a sense of purpose. When you feel hopeless and helpless, it's hard to experience happiness. We need a good purpose. It gives us something worthwhile to look forward to and fills us with energy and enthusiasm.

Eventually, my attitude began to shift, change, mold and form into the emotions caused by my circumstances. Point blank, I was negative. My attitude became toxic and unhelpful. I was miserable and my attitude was defeating and limiting any chance of success in any area of my life. And as you will learn in the following pages, when you choose to operate from a perspective of defeat, you produce more defeat. Your actions and choices reflect defeat. Remember, everything follows your attitude. If your attitude isn't right, your actions, behaviors and choices aren't going to follow in sync. Change your attitude and you change what follows.

I share more in depth about this story in previous books, but I was having a very bad day. A good friend invited me to coffee. Our coffee talk was me venting, complaining, blaming and filling up our space with my toxic attitude. Everything out of my mouth was about why things were bad and not getting better. It was a pity party, and I was the host.

My friend, calmly, took a deep breath. Took a sip of coffee, smiled and began to share words that would free me from a painful mental pattern of toxic thinking. My friend was very honest and caring when he communicated a simple truth, *"Sam, your life isn't lousy, but your attitude is. I know you don't want to hear that, but your attitude is that one thing that is preventing you from a better you and a better life. You have to change your attitude first, and everything will follow."*

We sat there for another hour drinking coffee and working through the junk in my life with a new plan, new thoughts and new choices. Sometimes, the junk just adds up over time and it doesn't just evaporate in an instant. We have to work through it. It's a process of growing. And it's not always easy.

While I consider this a moment in time that changed my life, it was an instant change. It took time to develop momentum and the thing is, I am still learning and growing. I don't think that ever goes away.

Having a better understanding of my attitude or awareness helped me changed my thoughts. Instead of feeding the pity party in my mind, I started by doing what worked during my college internship – reading good quotes and eventually good books. I changed the process of input. I became more intentional and aware of what I was inputting into my thinking.

As my attitude improved, so did so many areas of my life. Even though my attitude was on a better path, it didn't limit or stop the junk from happening in life, but rather it gave me a new way of dealing with the junk – a better way. Instead of allowing my thoughts to turn to junk when life gave me a junky situation, I used the next lesson to prevent my attitude from working against me. Read on...

Attitude Lesson #5
Be Aware of Your Attitude

How do you improve the quality of your attitude so that it rewards you?

AWARENESS.

The other day, I was sitting at the airport waiting for my flight to board and heard this couple talking. The wife said, "Harold, your butt is talking."

He said, "Oh, my stomach isn't feeling so great."

She smiled and said, "That isn't what I meant. Your butt is really talking. Your phone is in your back pocket, and I think you butt dialed someone. I can hear them talking."

Harold had no awareness that he butt dialed Walmart on the day he was having stomach issues. I couldn't stop laughing. But, we all have those moments when we our awareness isn't spot on. As you develop your awareness, you can also make healthy choices that help your attitude work for you. In fact, just this morning my daughter was treating everyone to an attitude of crankiness. I asked her if she had eaten anything, and she hadn't. She was hangry. Do you know anyone like that? I get like that at times and so, I always carry bars with me so my attitude doesn't spiral out of control because my body is hungry. This is awareness in action.

I was informing my daughter that when you feel this way, be aware of it and eat something. I said you don't want to go around spreading crankiness all day. She ate, she was happy and life was good again. But, as she develops this awareness as to what factors affect her attitude, she will be able take action to resolve the issue quicker instead of letting it linger out of control. This is the value of developed awareness.

Let's start with some simple questions to explain and explore your attitude awareness

- Is your attitude helping or hurting?

- Is your attitude more often in the way or making a way?

- Does your attitude mostly bring others down or lift them up?

- Would you call your attitude an asset or a liability? WHY?

- Does your attitude make relationships better or worse?

- What needs to change to make your attitude better?

- When you are tired, stressed and hungry, how does your attitude affect your life, human interactions and choices?

- Is there anything that triggers you to think, speak or act in a toxic way? What action can you take to address this so your negative emotions don't randomly grab the steering wheel of your life?

Really think about those questions, but also some solutions. The goal isn't perfection, but rather progress. What do you need to work on to improve your attitude awareness? What can you edit that would help you more?

For example, I know when I feel crazy stressed out, I paint. That is my go to option to find a better mindset or head space. In the professional world, we call it wellness. I call it fun! However, it works for me. So, the key is you have to determine what healthy options you can do that ensure your attitude resets, recharges and works for you.

Here is another way you can expand your attitude awareness - feedback.

How would others describe your attitude?

If you have kids, wow would your kids describe your attitude?

Don't be afraid to ask someone who cares about you, "Is there anything I can do better or work on?"

And then act on that.

Awareness for the Super Positive Attitudes

If you have a super positive attitude, that is super awesome. Understand this metric, people who don't have a great attitude aren't filling their Amazon carts with books like this. People who care about improving their life and the lives of others read books like this for fuel. You expand and strengthen your attitude awareness by fueling up.

	

Have you ever seen a car race like the Indianapolis 500? These incredibly and highly tuned cars race around a track for hours at high speeds. Every so often, they do what is known as a pit stop. They refuel, fix what needs fixing, change tires, eat a bucket of cheese – just kidding about the bucket of cheese. However, even though it may not seem like they are in the race, that pit stop is what strengthens the car and improves their chances of winning the race.

Think of your attitude like a race car. Every so often, you need to take a pit stop to refuel and in doing so, you improve your chances of winning in life.

When you have a great attitude, the goal is to elevate your attitude to a new level and experience life there. There is only one word that can describe this new level—better! Your life gets better as much as you get better and what makes that a reality is a better attitude. Awareness is remembering to keep feeding what works for you.

Awareness is Turning Off the Auto Pilot

Your attitude awareness is a time to self-reflect and redirect if needed. For example, when I feel overly stressed, I am tempted to eat sweets. If there is sugar, I want it! This awareness helps me redirect my attitude, so I make better choices. Awareness can break long standing bad habits, so look at it as self-care. This is what brings your life value—you are looking out for you in a good way.

And let's be real, nobody wants to hear that their attitude isn't working for them. But, instead of putting your head down in frustration, see it as an opportunity. It's not a bad thing so don't view it like that; it just may mean you need a little tune-up. This is how you nurture and develop a healthy and rewarding attitude.

Awareness turns the autopilot off and puts you in the driver's seat. If you leave your attitude to CHANCE, the consequences can actually make a bumpy road bumpier. Your attitude can give you resilience on a bumpy road or create massive potholes that make the journey unhealthy. Some people have no idea or clue that their biggest hurdle in life is not being in tune with how their attitude authentically affects their life.

You will be taking a big risk if you are not tuned into how your attitude is functioning. Our attitudes are incredibly vulnerable to influences, energies, vibes, and circumstances. So, paying attention to what is influencing or feeding your attitude will strengthen and expand the quality of your awareness. Awareness is paying attention to your thoughts or what is feeding your thinking. To think better, you have to input better content into your mind. For example, if you sit around and watch the news for hours, have you ever noticed that your vocabulary and thinking begin to mirror the same information? The lesson here is being aware that as you immerse yourself in whatever, your attitude will reflect it and take on the form of it.

By opening the door to greater awareness, you empower yourself with options to make helpful edits or healthy changes.

I have been researching and studying the topic of attitude for three decades, but I never wake up in the morning and announce, "Well, I know it all, so I am set for the day."

My focus is betterment and progress. That should be your goal as well. Be willing to grow your awareness and make improvements that empower you to be and live your best. So, the next question is how do you build a better attitude?

Attitude Lesson #6
Think a Little Better and Life Becomes Significantly Better

THINK BETTER.

Those two words are life-changing if you allow them to be.

Think better.

When we think better, we make better choices.

When we think better, we act better.

We do better.

We feel better.

However, thinking better is not solely a process of thinking positively. If you were in a hurricane, I would never say, "It's going to be okay, just think positive!"

That just doesn't work.

To get to a place of thinking optimistically, you have to think better first. I am all for the positive feelings and emotions that come from positivity, but always thinking positively is hard, challenging, and unrealistic. However, thinking better is possible, doable, and more impactful.

So, how do we think better?

I think a good place to start is by reflecting on the moments you didn't think or do too well. Let me ask you, can you think of a time when the attitude you brought to a situation made the situation much worse? Have you ever thought, "Oh, I could have handled that better?"

I can relate. I think we all can. Those are not feel-good moments, but those moments help us grow in a way that we learn and improve. As a result, we gain the experience and wisdom that some may lack.

We will not always have a perfect and positive attitude, but we can always focus on getting a little better and allowing progress to create positive momentum for us. This is achievable and very realistic.

Another idea to help you think better is determining what helps you think better. What is your formula for balancing your thoughts and emotions so you feel better?

Maybe it's talking to someone and venting. Or it could be as simple as going for a 15-minute walk, taking a long hot shower, or engaging in my favorite— a good nap. Could it be a good cup of coffee and a good book? What about a funny movie? I love movies that make me laugh and feel good.

We all have different things that contribute to our well-being. So, let me return to the process of awareness. If you are having a tough day, knowing or being aware of what puts you back on a better path is preparation for better thinking. For example, I paint for my wellness. You can check out my artwork online. In fact, I post my art weekly on Facebook. I am not the world's greatest artist, but I don't mind. I love painting for fun. It puts me in a mindset that I can think more clearly. It calms me so I am not reactive to things I cannot control. I know that when I am having a tough day, feeling overwhelmed, and needing an escape, going to my studio to paint for 30 minutes helps me think better.

I learned how to think better through discovery. For years, I would reach for sugar and binge eat unhealthy food to cope with anxiety and stress. I got tired of being reactive to what I call "Life Uncontrollables."

My awareness communicated that I needed to make changes to my thinking. It's not always an overnight snap of your fingers; life is a perfect kind of process. It's a process, but once you develop momentum in that process, it becomes wind to your sail.

When I identified the activities I could do when I wasn't thinking my best, I knew what I could turn to that would help ease me back into a better head space. When I did this, I stopped damaging my body with unhealthy food. The key to thinking better is taking a moment to identify what makes you think and feel better in a healthy way. When life trips you up with a bad day or challenging situation, knowing what helps you think better will be a tool that can save you from a lot of pain. Remember this, as I share it often in my speeches and books, "A better or positive attitude isn't going to stop the junk from happening in your life. Stuff happens. That is a fact. However, a better attitude will give you the mental endurance, resilience, and creativity to deal with the junk, learn from it, use it, and grow from it."

The last thought on thinking better is that it has valuable benefits! When you think better, you are better for your family. When you think better, you lead better, parent better, care for yourself better, and become a better person to be around.

Thinking better makes us more optimistic and resilient in situations challenging us to lose our cool. Honestly, it just takes a little practice.

Here is a little story that will encourage you to think better when things are not going your way.

The Greatest Hitter in the World

A little boy was overheard talking to himself as he strutted through the backyard, wearing his baseball cap, and toting a ball and bat. "I'm the greatest hitter in the world," he announced. Then he tossed the ball into the air, swung at it, and missed. "Strike One!" he yelled. Undaunted, he picked up the ball and said again, "I'm the greatest hitter in the world!" He tossed the ball into the air. When it came down, he swung again and missed. "Strike Two!" he cried. The boy then paused a moment to scrutinize his bat and ball. He straightened his cap and said again, "I'm the greatest hitter in the world!" Again, he tossed the ball up in the air and swung at it. And again, he missed. "Strike Three! Wow!" the boy exclaimed. "I'm the greatest pitcher in the world!"

What a fun story and reminder that you make your life better when you think a little better.

My Top 3 Ways to Think Better

1. Practice. (Practice makes improvement, not perfection.)

2. Learn from your lessons. (Think about when you didn't think so great and what you could have done differently, and it will equip you to think better and do better the next time a similar circumstance pops up.)

3. Be Intentional. (Re-read Chapter 1 or Attitude Lesson #1. What you feed your attitude is what it becomes. Be intentional about feeding your thoughts what helps them grow into better thoughts.)

Attitude Lesson #7
Your Attitude is Your Interpreter

My family loves watching the birds fill up our backyard with their playfulness and beauty. One day my daughter was looking out the back window and said, "I don't know if the birds are going to visit us anymore."

I inquired, "Why?"

"Well, Daddy, everything is so dirty out there."

I examined what she was seeing, got some window cleaner, and washed the dirt off the outside window. And just like that, the view changed.

My daughter said, "Daddy, I think that did the job! It looks so much better now. I think the birds will be happy to visit us now."

I only washed the window, and the perception and interpretation changed.

Our attitude is the window into our world. It determines how we interpret information as well as our circumstances. Whatever happens around you, your attitude always filters and determines what to do with the data. Sometimes our attitude filters have been taught to us by our influences growing up—friends, family, and even the media. If your parents always looked for the negative in everything, there is a good chance you may have picked that up from them. If you recognize that and are aware of it, you can work on breaking that mental pattern and develop an attitude that looks for the silver lining in situations.

You might ask, is it a bad thing to look for a silver lining when things go wrong?

NO WAY! Looking for an unseen benefit and using it to your advantage is one of the smartest things you can do. It's not turning a blind eye to what might be a difficult circumstance, but rather that positive aspect can be used for strength and resourcefulness. A silver lining can be rocket fuel to keep going when everything and everyone communicates, "give up."

I do think it is especially important to avoid toxic positivity. Life touches us all differently, and those experiences come with unique emotions. Those emotions don't go away instantly. Sometimes, they stay with you and teach you lessons. I discovered years ago; it is literally possible to be in two places simultaneously in your thinking. When my grandfather passed away, I was sad and happy at the same time. I was sad he was no longer with us, but happy that I got the time I did with him. These were emotions I had to address and learn from.

There are times in life when things happen that knock us off our mental feet, and it feels like no matter how hard you try to think positively or do things to feel better, nothing works. I get it. The journey to dealing with experiences and emotions is a personal one. Some thoughts, feelings, and emotions can feel like we just stepped into a pothole. You might feel numb, angry, or annoyed and not understand why. Still, the process of healing, getting better, and learning to manage those unfavorable or unexpected emotions can make us stronger, more resilient, and wiser. So, hear me clearly when I say it is a process of growth and betterment. It isn't an instant coffee fix. Some things take time, and that is okay. You don't have to rush or feel pressured to move on instantly. Embrace the experience of your emotions and learn from them.

Improving the quality of your thinking and interpretation of less-than-ideal circumstances requires PRACTICE.

What you practice repeatedly becomes a habit. I realized we might not have the best of things, but with a better attitude, we can make the best of things, and with just that one edit and shift, I have changed the entire experience. It was a process that wasn't forced. It was a choice to engage in the process of finding a better way of making things better.

Even though my art studio is smaller, I am having more fun than ever doing art. We have a beautiful home in a safe neighborhood. We have more to celebrate than complain about. Are there weeds in this picture? Oh yeah, but I choose not to let the weeds overtake my thinking. And again, this takes practice.

Give it a try. Practice what you want to improve on. When things are less than ideal, I am not saying, "Okay, ignore the situation and think happy thoughts, Peter Pan!" That won't work. But, if you can find a good place in your thinking, you will find a place to build on. You can nurture it, feed it, and use it to your advantage. This will allow you to think more peacefully, creatively, and resourcefully.

Attitude Lesson #8
Free Yourself from Overthinking

If there is one thing that trips us up in life, it's overthinking. Overthinking causes added stress, anxiety, and fear. Overthinking comes from thinking you must control everything or worry about how to handle everything going on in your life. Have you ever struggled to fall asleep at night because your mind wouldn't turn off? Your mind jumps from one thing to another and as a result you become mentally exhausted and burned out. I have been there many times, so I get it. I understand. The question is how do we shift our mind so it's not operating like a pinball machine that won't turn off?

What I am about to share with you may seem overly simplistic. I thought it was when I first heard it, but the more I thought about it, the more I realized, it worked. For myself, I just wanted some freedom from feeling out of control, from anxiety, and the fear of uncertainty and the unexpected.

The truth is, there is a lot we cannot control in life. Throwing worry, anxiety, and fear on top of that doesn't help. We know that. You know that. But still our mind shifts in that overthinking mode, and we feel helpless or out of control.

The other day, I heard a fantastic analogy about being lost in a highly wooded forest without a clear path out. When we focus on everything in the way, we feed worry, stress, and fear into our thought process. Then panic sets in because we don't see a way out or a path out of the forest.

However, the analogy continued by encouraging us to focus only on the next step. By doing this, we shrink the dynamics of the situation, shift our focus to a more micro solution, and take one step at a time. When we focus on one thousand steps out of a forest, we experience every aspect of worry, fear, and stress. And, sometimes our imagination jumps into the mix by filling in the blanks with potential unrealized problems, therefore leading us down a path of overthinking.

It's a fact that what we focus on expands and grows. You must practice focusing on the immediate next step instead of the next one hundred steps. I say practice because your practice will strengthen the habit, so when you feel tempted to overthink, you immediately shift gears and think in a way that calms you and frees you from overthinking.

So, how do you shift your focus, so you are not overthinking?

Here are a few helpful tips.

1. Give your mind a 15-minute break.

When we overthink, we experience unthinkable feelings and emotions. So, take a break. Take a break when you feel like you are starting to overthink anything. Have you ever noticed when your mind is stuck on overthinking mode, you tend to be more reactive, agitated, triggered, and even moody towards others?

You need a break. Sit, walk, move, or do whatever gives you a mild distraction from feeding your mind with more stressful thoughts. I like to call it, stop feeding the fire. Take a few deep breaths and simply focus on your breathing. The goal is to relax as best as you can and calm your mind so it's not racing a million miles a minute. A 15-minute break is enough time to be aware, act, and change the direction of your thoughts. It may not solve every problem in your life, but it's enough time to take your eyes off the heavily wooded forest and focus on the next step.

For me, I do art and go for walks. Those work for me. Find something that works for you that is healthy. It recharges you, rekindles what makes you shine, and makes you smile again.

2. Rest.

Rest is taking a longer break. Specifically, get some real sleep. You are not going to think your best when you are exhausted. I am not advocating to be lazy, but rather to be more intentional about resting in a way that renews your mind to a better place of thinking.

I have been traveling for years and that means my schedule can have me going in every direction. Sometimes, I don't check into a hotel until late and then I have to be up and on my A game early in the morning. I can do this occasionally, just not every day. Over the years, I have adjusted my travel to allow time to rest. So, I may arrive a day early before a speaking engagement or leave a day later. The advantage for me when I am rested is that I make better choices. For example, when I am rested, I make better food choices. When I am overly tired, I don't really think about eating healthy. I might eat to eat and that isn't healthy. When I am rested, I feel better, think better, treat myself better, treat others better, and have more energy to do more of what I desire in life.

The key is you must create a sleep routine that gives you the right amount of rest. As much as I love coffee, you can't rely 100% on it to keep you mentally energized.

The more you practice a healthy sleep routine, the more you will notice your energy will go up, but your thinking will improve also. An exhausted mind is one that becomes vulnerable to overthinking. This way of life is not healthy. If you need to make some changes that allow you to get enough rest so you can think and live better, then you need to work on developing the habit through practice.

3. Talk to someone you trust.

Sometimes, we just need to talk it out to get it out. Talking to a professional or someone close is very healthy. Suppressing thoughts that cause overthinking is very unhealthy.

Talking to someone that cares for you is very empowering—even life changing. For myself, it's gaining a better perspective on things. In fact, there are certain people in my life, that just talking with them about "whatever and anything" makes me feel more at peace. This can even be that 15-minute break I mentioned.

I think it's good to have someone you can be real with regarding your battles, fears, and struggles. It's the process of finding strength when you feel weak, lost, or even scared. Having someone to bounce thoughts off relieves the pressure of overthinking. Talking with someone that doesn't judge us but accepts us and supports us helps bring us back to a place of focusing on life's next step versus the next one hundred steps.

Remember, don't feel bad when you do overthink. Rather use it as a learning opportunity and practice being more aware of what happens when you do and how you feel. This awareness becomes your opportunity to make a quick change—a healthy change for the better. We all slip into an overthinking rut from time to time and the best thing you can do for you is to determine what calms your mind so it's not racing in one hundred different directions.

Attitude Lesson #9
You cannot change anyone's attitude; only your own

Recently, I finished giving my most requested speech, *"Attitude Changes Everything."* It's a fun talk filled with art, humor, and great insights. I was doing a meet and greet, and this really nice woman shared with me, "Sam, this is the third time I have seen you speak. I purchased all your books and gave them away as gifts to my family. They all got offended, and some of them won't even talk to me anymore. I thought they would enjoy the books as much I did, but they didn't see it that way."

I was sad to hear this, but her intentions were golden. I would say that most of the people who buy my books purchase extras to give away. When something feels good and is a great experience, you want to give that same gift to others—especially the ones you love.

However, remember the last chapter on interpretation. Some people won't see the good that you see in things. Instead of seeing a book as something fun and happy, they will take offense to it as, "So you are saying there is something wrong with my attitude?"

I once had a gentleman introduce me before my speech saying, "Our speaker today is going to talk a lot about attitude, but it's not because you have an attitude problem."

A little side note. If you ever have a speaker on attitude or I am a guest speaker at your event, trust me when I tell you, IT IS A GIFT. And for those who know me, have seen me, or follow my work, you know that is the truth.

So, how do you fix someone else's attitude if it isn't working right?

The bad news: You can't.

The good news: You can go through the process of influence, encouragement, and example.

Years ago, I attended a networking event, and I was asked what I do for a living.

"I am a professional motivational speaker and bestselling author who inspires the audience to think better so they lead and live better."

Several people inquired about the titles of my books. So, I said, "The Gift of Attitude, A Kick in the Attitude, Attitude is a Choice, and Attitude Changes Everything."

It's easy to spot the theme of my work. One woman boldly said, "I don't need to read books on attitude, I have a good one!"

Everyone just had bewildered looks on their face. This woman said it in such a way as if she were defending her attitude. I kindly responded, "Good for you!"

She continued to speak up and share all the reasons why she didn't need to read books about attitude and why they are a waste of time.

Here is a little awareness. It is a red flag when someone announces they have a positive attitude, and it is a bigger red flag when they defend why they don't need to read books that help them think better.

People with a better attitude don't speak like that. That is not the language of someone who properly cares for their attitude. A person with an average, negative, or apathetic attitude isn't in line at a bookstore investing in books that will improve their life or work. Sometimes, they operate on the assumption that everyone else is negative.

A healthy attitude is displayed through action. There is no need to announce or prove it. However, here is something that will give you perspective on the difference between a healthy attitude and one that may not be. A person with a healthy attitude relies on books, audio, videos, mentors, and coaches to keep their attitude healthy. Those things are fuel for your mental health. Your attitude needs food. If you are not feeding your mind good stuff, it is probably starving for something good.

When you feed your attitude something good, it puts muscle on your attitude—the kind of muscle that empowers you to think resiliently and optimistically when life bombards you with changes, challenges, uncertainty, and negative situations and people.

A healthy attitude relies on fuel to keep it strong. Without fuel, your attitude becomes weak and vulnerable to toxic forms such as worry, fear, anger, and reaction.

So, when you encounter someone with an attitude you know isn't working for them, the best way to help them is to be an example, encourage them, and be influential.

How do you do this?

Here are a few tips that will help.

1. Establish boundaries.

A negative person may not respond to common sense or reason. You can try and reason with them, but if you do, be prepared that they may not understand or respond to your logic very well. So, for example, if they are complaining about something, ask them if they found anything positive in the situation or circumstance. If you feel they are not responding to logic, it's best to interrupt them and excuse yourself. This is you creating a boundary to limit your time with them. The more you listen to it, the more they vent their negativity. As I like to say, don't engage the rage because what you tolerate is what you promote. They will soon grasp that you are not an ear for their negativity.

Limit your time with negative people. You may have a family member or work with someone who rides the negative train to and from work daily. You need to find a way to limit your time with them. Is it healthy to be dragged down daily by someone's negative ways? NO. In fact, I once interrupted someone, asked if they could get a tic tac, and made a gesture that their breath smelled—it worked! They stopped venting and complaining and unloading their negativity on me. They really had a stinky attitude, and I didn't have time to bat their negativity back and forth like I was in a ping-pong match.

Remember, a boundary is a communicator. This is an example and influence. It lets others know you do not wish to participate in what isn't healthy or promote it. There is a difference between listening to someone having a bad day and offering encouragement versus listening to someone whose every encounter is draining, toxic, and filled with complaining, blaming, and gossip. You have the discernment to know the difference. We all can have bad days, but you can't participate in party planning with those who choose to make every day bad. Make sense?

2. Do your best to be kind and calm the situation down if it escalates.

Keep your cool. Stay professional, keep your composure, and don't reciprocate in a negative way when someone is speaking or acting negatively. When someone is stuck in a bad state of mind, they may say or do something hurtful. Realize that throwing dirt back at them isn't going to put things in a good place. Stay calm and communicate calmly and see if you can lead them to a better place of thinking.

3. Don't try to change them.

You can be an influence for healthy change, but ultimately, people have to choose to give up being unhealthy. You cannot do that for them. However, it helps to have a good heart-to-heart conversation and communicate honestly how their unhealthy attitude and actions are hurtful and unhelpful.

They may listen and change if they trust you and know you care. Back to the start of the book, I told you about my cup of coffee with a friend who confronted me about my attitude. I could have thrown my hot coffee at him, but I opened my mind and heart to his feedback, which changed my life... for the better.

Attitude Lesson #10
The Most Life Changing Attitude in Existence is Gratitude

It was 10 am, and I was about to give a speech to over six hundred hospital employees. This hospital was hosting an employee recognition event. It was an opportunity to express gratitude for working hard. The event was catered with great food, decorations, awards, and prizes. I was the guest speaker hired to encourage, inspire, and recharge their attitude batteries. They had been experiencing burnout and stress, and my goal was to relieve them.

As I stood in the back, waiting to be introduced, I conversed with the CEO. And then he asked me this, "Sam, do you really think events like this make a difference?"

I looked at him and said, "Imagine the difference it would make if you did nothing.

He nodded and smiled in agreement and understanding.

The message was clear; gratitude is the highest form of recognition.

I once heard a saying that gratitude turns crumbs into a feast. When we are filled with gratitude, we are kinder, more caring, loving, and happier people.

Allow me to share how to make gratitude more powerful in your life.

I think there are moments in the day worth pausing and allowing yourself to be in the moment and reflect on what you have to be grateful for. If you can make this a habit, it has a way of putting a little strength in your attitude. It also empowers your mindset to look and hunt for what is good. Whatever your mind sets out to look for, it will find. Because of these, seeking out things to be grateful for will help you minimize complaining. So, if your mind is hunting for things to be grateful for, you will have less time hunting for things to complain about. Right?

I finished a speaking engagement a few years ago, and I know I am my worst critic, but I didn't feel like it went well. I was frustrated with the sound system. If the sound system is off, it can minimize how well you connect and communicate. The sound guy wasn't in the room, and nobody knew how to fix it, so I had to do my best. However, everything felt off.

When I got to the airport to head home, I found a coffee shop to sit and stew in my frustrations. I kept shaking my head about the situation. But then something happened, and my pity party started to grow. I complained about everything in my life, "Why this, why that, on and on.

I looked down at my coffee and thought, I may need something stronger. I was spiraling fast. But then something happened—a reminder. Gratitude offers reminders that bring us back to a place of reasonable and balanced thinking.

I looked over at the woman sitting at the table next to me. She was smiling. She smiled in a way that communicated, "Life is as good as much as you want it to be."

Her friend sitting next to her assisted by lifting her coffee cup and helping her drink, adding to her smile. Then, the picture came into focus. She had no arms.

Here I am, stewing over a bad sound system, and this person has no arms but is happier than me. And here is a compelling perspective on having gratitude. Sometimes, it's not about reflecting on what you are grateful for, but rather what you are grateful you do not have.

Did my attitude change at that moment? Yes, it did. I left my pity party and realized that my minor negatives have no power over me in the presence of my major positives. I wasn't thinking about them then because I was hyper-focused on feeding my negatives.

But here is something you need to understand about gratitude. You feel the experience and power that comes from gratitude when you don't force it the wrong way. For example, if someone you love is having a tough day, it is probably not the best idea to say, "Hey, get over it; someone has it one hundred times worse than you!" Or say, "Well, let's sit down and write out one hundred things to be grateful for."

Forcing something that may work for you may not work for others. So, it's not a great idea to force gratitude. Let the process be organic. Once we get a better place of thinking, we experience the effects of gratitude more.

Some people might say that if you are having a bad day, stop what you are doing and be grateful. My honest advice is that sometimes this works, and sometimes it doesn't. There are some days that I know I have much to be grateful for, but I still feel lousy anyway. And there is nothing wrong with that. It's called being human. The key is that you don't want the process of connecting to gratitude to be toxic. You want it to be powerful and meaningful. Gratitude is an attitude. It is an experience. It is a perspective that can change how we see and approach the world. The process of getting to that state of gratitude is just that—a process of practice and awareness. On days I don't feel my best, I would still try my best to do something, which helps connect to the strength of gratitude. I am not trying to force something to work because I read it in a book or blog or heard it on a podcast. I am working to find what works for me so my connection to gratitude is authentic and meaningful.

Expressing gratitude is one of the highest forms of love and recognition. It communicates, "I see you. I value you. I care about you."

Some people have no idea how incredible they are until you tell them. Expressing gratitude can be as simple as using these two underused words, "Thank you."

I remember one of my first jobs out of college, my supervisor always wrote a little note on everyone's paycheck. It was a handwritten note expressing gratitude: "Sam, I know you had a crazy week, but I sure appreciate how you kept the right attitude and used that to make it a great week for yourself and your co-workers."

Those little handwritten letters inspired me. Gratitude expressed in little ways equals a big impact. In fact, the more grateful you are, the less power entitlement has. I remember being in line at the grocery store, and the person behind me had fewer items, so naturally, I said, *"Please, go in front of me, you have less."*

Her response was riddled with entitlement, *"Well, I would think so!"*

I assumed my small act of kindness might warrant a simple response of gratitude but was instead met with entitlement. This experience taught me a valuable lesson—not everyone will think like you. Not everyone understands how to be, express, or create an experience of gratitude. I was trying to be kind by letting the person go in front of me, but also create an experience of gratitude for them, like the person who paid for my coffee in front of me at Starbucks. When you encounter entitlement, don't let it influence you. Sure, it doesn't feel great, but let it go... fast! The danger is if you let entitlement take root in your attitude, you will only be hunting for what makes you unhappy. Entitled people experience more unhappiness than they do authentic joy and gratitude. And this is sad.

Also, be aware of this. It is great to express gratitude but don't let others take advantage of you. The experience of gratitude is a gift, but some people will try to take all you have until there is nothing left but bitterness. Don't let them. Don't let them manipulate you or take advantage of you to the point where you have nothing left to give.

And finally, recognize, reward, and reinforce whatever you want to see more in the world. The other day I stood in line at the grocery store and noticed the gentleman in front of me saying to the cashier, "You always have such an amazing smile. I love shopping here to see you smile."

WOW! A few kind words made that cashier's day. She was so grateful that her smile doubled in size. What I witnessed is what gratitude is all about. It's an experience that recognizes something special and rewards it with a few kind words that reinforce it.

Let me ask you this, do you think when it was my turn to check out, I was treated to one of those super smiles? I sure was!

I, too, participated in the gratitude experience by saying, "That guy is right. You have a million-dollar smile!"

An attitude of gratitude is a game-changer in life.

In Closing

I hope you got a few helpful insights into how incredibly dynamic your attitude is and what a significant role it plays in your life and work. Remember, the keys that will help you the most are to be intentional, be aware, and practice choosing an attitude that rewards and works for you.

The most important thing to walk away with is that your attitude isn't something that has to be perfect but something that can always keep improving. So, value your progress. Embrace it. Take small steps every day and develop those habits that make the process of improving your attitude and life something to look forward to instead of just another thing to add to the to-do list. Make the process and routine of getting better a joyful experience.

Keep looking up, and remember, I am rooting for you!

Sam Glenn

The Attitude Guy

www.SamGlenn.com

#ACE – Attitude Changes Everything

"The difference between an

average day and an

awesome day is the attitude

you choose every day."

- Sam Glenn.

#ACE

9 789693 792218